Targeting Comprehension

Year 4

Peter Alford and Aimee Bloom

PASCAL

Targeting Comprehension Year 4

Copyright © 2020 Blake Education
Reprinted 2021, 2022
ISBN 978 1 925490 63 3

Published by Pascal Press
PO Box 250
Glebe NSW 2037
contact@pascalpress.com.au

Authors: Peter Alford and Aimee Bloom
Publisher: Lynn Dickinson
Editor: Marie Theodore
Typesetter: Stacey Grainger
Series consultant: Del Merrick
Printed by Wai Man Book Binding (China) Ltd

AUSTRALIAN CURRICULUM CORRELATIONS: English

YEAR FOUR

LITERACY

Interpreting, Analysing and Evaluating
Identify characteristic features used in imaginative, informative and persuasive texts to meet the purpose of the text (ACELY1690)
Use comprehension strategies to build literal and inferred meaning to expand content knowledge, integrating and linking ideas and analysing and evaluating texts (ACELY1692)

LITERATURE

Examining Literature
Discuss how authors and illustrators make stories exciting, moving and absorbing and hold readers' interest by using various techniques, for example character development and plot tension (ACELT1605)

Contents

• HOW TO USE THIS BOOK •

A good understanding of comprehension is essential for effective writing and communication. This book gives you the skills to read between the lines. It contains activities for Literal and Inferential comprehension.

Literal comprehension is simply understanding exactly what the text says. Inferential comprehension is more complicated as it requires you to interpret ideas, intent or information in the text and to make assumptions. The activities in this book are intended to teach you how to unpick texts so that you can understand all the meanings embedded in them. In other words — how to read between the lines.

Inferential comprehension can be divided up into the following elements and each of them has their own sections in this book. They are explained using a variety of informative, imaginative and persuasive sample texts. The different elements are:

- **Literal** – understanding information and facts directly stated in the text
- **Inferring** – making assumptions based on context
- **Predicting** – imagining where aspects of a text may lead
- **Analysing** – interpreting the ideas behind what is written
- **Making connections** – finding links between two elements of a text
- **Critical reflection** – drawing on your own experience and knowledge to understand characters

Also included is an assessment section for each of the six comprehension elements and removable answers. Australian Curriculum correlations can be found on page ii.

Quick Guide to:

• LITERAL COMPREHENSION •

Franklin the dog bounded up the hill, through the tall, green grass. His owner, Ali, ran quickly behind him.

"Look at that view!" Ali exclaimed. "I've never seen a more beautiful sunset."

Ali sighed happily and sat on the grass. Franklin looked at Ali before running around in little circles and sniffing the grass. Finally finding what he was looking for, Franklin proudly bounced over to his owner with a stick in his mouth.

"I don't know where you get all your energy from!" laughed Ali. "OK, let's play fetch again."

Some questions about a text require you to find an answer in what you have read. The answer will be the exact words the writer had written. These questions are **literal questions.**

Example of a literal question:

What did Franklin find in the grass?

Answer: He found a stick.

Answers to **literal questions** are always the exact words used by the writer. There is only one correct answer and it is always found right there on the page.

Example of a literal question:

Ali thought the view was beautiful. What was she looking at?

Answer: Ali was looking at the beautiful sunset.

DID YOU NOTICE?

The answer to a **literal question** can be found directly in the text. It is written right there on the page.

Franklin ran around frantically — he'd lost his best friend. One minute, Franklin had been playing happily, growling, sniffing, chewing — all his favourite dog things to do. The next minute, his owner, Chris, had called him away. And now, Franklin's friend had disappeared.

Franklin ran in ever-increasing circles, searching everywhere. On the couch? No. Behind the chair? No. Franklin began to whimper and cry — where had his friend gone and why couldn't Franklin find him?

Ali, Franklin's other owner, saw his panicked movements. "Franklin!" she called. "What are you looking for?" Franklin looked at Ali and then continued to sniff the floor in every direction.

"You're not looking for this are you?" Ali held up the rubber chicken she had been cleaning in the sink. Franklin looked up at Ali and started jumping up and down, barking happily. "Whoever would have thought a rubber chicken could be a dog's best friend?" Ali laughed.

1 True or False? Franklin is a dog.

☐ True ☐ False

2 What are Franklin's favourite things to do? Tick the correct answer.

a) growl, bark and run ☐

b) jump, bark and sniff ☐

c) chew, sniff and bark ☐

d) growl, sniff and chew ☐

3 Why was Franklin upset?

____

____

____

TARGETING COMPREHENSION 4 © PASCAL PRESS ISBN 9781925490633

4 Tick the box next to the statement that you think is the most accurate answer.

a) Franklin liked to run in the house and sniff things. ☐
b) Franklin was sniffing so he could find his friend. ☐
c) Franklin was running and sniffing because he is a dog. ☐
d) Franklin was sniffing to find some food. ☐

5 Colour the items (nouns) that are mentioned in the story.

couch	bowl	lead
collar	chicken	friend
sink	chair	treat

6 Why did Ali have Franklin's friend? Tick the correct answer.

a) Ali was hiding Franklin's friend. ☐
b) Ali didn't like Franklin's friend. ☐
c) Ali was cleaning Franklin's friend. ☐
d) Franklin and Ali have the same friend. ☐

7 Circle the words that best describe Franklin's mood when he found his friend.

happy   sad   upset   joyful   worried   glad

8 True or False? This story has a happy ending.

☐ True   ☐ False

LITERAL

Erosion occurs when rocks or soil are worn away and moved. Erosion is mostly caused by water, wind and ice.

Physical erosion often involves rocks getting smaller or smoother. For example, water running over rocks in a creek or river can make the rocks bump into each other and become smooth over time; or a landslide can cause rocks to become loose and crumble as they fall down a slope.

Liquid erosion is the main form of erosion where bits of soil and sand are carried away by rivers, rain, creeks, floods and lakes.

Wind erosion can blow sand into towering dunes in the desert, or blast sand against rocks and wear them away.

Ice can erode the earth as massive slow-moving glaciers transport everything in their path, including rocks and soil.

1 Erosion occurs when rocks or soil are ______________ away and ______________ by wind or water.

2 What are the three most common causes of erosion?

a) physical erosion, liquid erosion, wind erosion ☐

b) water, wind and ice ☐

c) rivers, wind and glaciers ☐

3 What type of erosion makes rocks smaller or smoother?

____

TARGETING COMPREHENSION 4 © PASCAL PRESS ISBN 9781925490633

LITERAL

4 How could a flood cause erosion?

5 True or False? Wind erosion can involve sand wearing away rock.

☐ True ☐ False

6 Draw and label a picture showing one type of erosion.

LITERAL

SOCCER RULES!

Soccer is the best game to play. You can get fit, make friends and learn new skills.

Some kids think that playing with a phone or an iPad is the best way to spend their time. However, they don't realise that sitting down for most of the day won't make their bodies healthy. We kids need at least 60 minutes of running around in order for our hearts to be healthy. We also need to use our muscles in order to become stronger and have healthy bones.

Running is a great way to get our hearts healthy. Professional soccer players can run over 11 kilometres in just one game! Running is also a great activity for building healthy bones, meaning that playing soccer is even good for your skeleton.

By joining a soccer team, you are also joining a group of people who can become good friends. They need to work together to play well and often spend time together, training during the week and playing at the weekend. Spending time together and enjoying the same activities are two great ways to become friends with people.

Learning to play soccer will give you new and improved skills such as dribbling a ball and passing it to others, shielding the ball from the other team and tackling players to keep them from getting the ball. You'll also learn how to kick goals and you might even like to try goalkeeping.

We all need to keep our bodies healthy and strong, so why not give soccer a go? After all, who doesn't want more friends?

1 How much exercise does a kid your age need every day? Tick the correct answer.

a) 90 minutes ☐

b) 60 minutes ☐

c) 11 kilometres ☐

2 Why is soccer good for your heart?

____

____

____

TARGETING COMPREHENSION 4 © PASCAL PRESS ISBN 9781925490633

3 True or False? Running can help you to build healthy bones.

☐ True ☐ False

4 Name two ways to make new friends.

a) ______________________________

b) ______________________________

5 Circle the verbs (action words) used in the text.

playing	trapping	sitting
shooting	running	practising
dribbling	passing	winning

6 List five skills you can learn by playing soccer.

____

____

____

____

____

7 What are the three main reasons the author thinks soccer is a good game to play?

a) ______________________________

b) ______________________________

c) ______________________________

Quick Guide to:

INFERRING

The four killers surrounded Bertie who had built up some speed in fear for his life. Gnar got closer and closer followed by the biggest killer of the pod. They opened their mouths, showing their sharp pointed teeth. Gnar suddenly changed direction and torpedoed in at Bertie's flipper. Bertie swung his mighty tail and smacked the killer across the face, knocking him out of the water. He landed many metres away.

Answering questions about text often means finding the answer in what you have read. Sometimes you are asked to remember what was in the text. These are **literal** questions.

Example of a literal question:
In the sample text above, the story tells about a whale fighting for his life. How did the whale protect himself?

Answer: Whales have a mighty tail and the whale swung this at the killers.

Unlike literal questions, when you **infer**, the answers are not in the text. You have to guess the answer by using information in the text. **Inferring** is guessing, using what you already know.

Example of an inferring question:
What the 'killers' are, is not explained in the text. What do you think they are? What words helped you to guess your answer?

Answer: The 'killers' were killer whales because the text used the word 'pod'. Pod is the word for a group of whales.

DID YOU NOTICE?

The answer to the question is not in the text. You have to look for clues to **infer (guess)** the answer by using the words. To do this, you need to know about the word 'pod'. Pod is the name of a group of whales, therefore the 'killers' are killer whales.

TARGETING COMPREHENSION 4 © PASCAL PRESS ISBN 9781925490633

Mr and Mrs Kent lived in a lovely, little, old cottage. They had a big dam and a little creek with willow trees along the banks. In the dam lived fish and yabbies. The creek was covered with water iris blooms. On one side of the house was a cottage garden, bright with flowers. In the shrubs nearby, green tree frogs clung to leaves.

Behind the house was an enormous shed with all sorts of interesting things in it. But here and there, in fact just about everywhere, weeds and grass and rubbishy plants, such as fireweed, sprouted madly.

Then something happened. Something totally unexpected! Someone gave Mr and Mrs Kent two goats. "Goats eat almost anything," said Mr Kent.

Source: Gigglers, *The Goats*, Blake Education. [abridged]

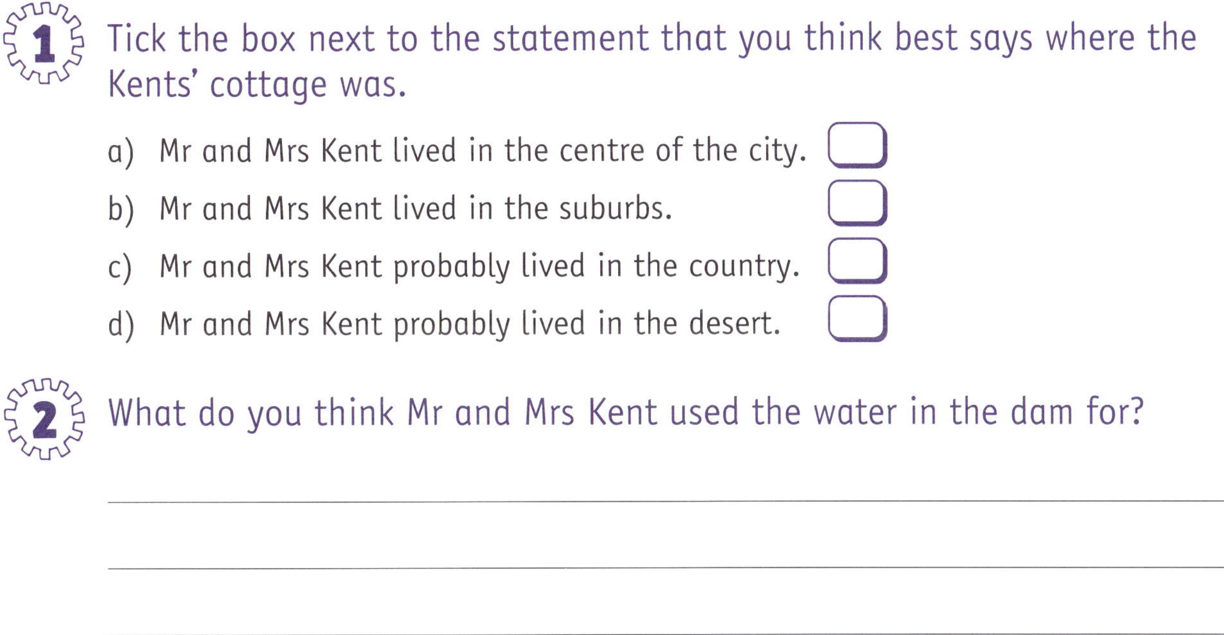

1. Tick the box next to the statement that you think best says where the Kents' cottage was.

   a) Mr and Mrs Kent lived in the centre of the city. ☐
   b) Mr and Mrs Kent lived in the suburbs. ☐
   c) Mr and Mrs Kent probably lived in the country. ☐
   d) Mr and Mrs Kent probably lived in the desert. ☐

2. What do you think Mr and Mrs Kent used the water in the dam for?

____

____

____

3. What do you think Mr and Mrs Kent did with the fish and yabbies from the dam? Colour the face of the correct answer.

   a) The Kents kept them as pets and trained them. 
   b) The Kents caught them and cooked them for dinner. 
   c) The Kents kept them as friends for the goats. 

INFERRING

4 Colour the things that you think were in the shed. Clue: The cottage had lots of gardens and land around it.

tools	cake mixer	garden tools
blankets	lawn mower	computer
food	old bikes	goldfish

5 Explain why you chose **one** of the words you coloured. What clues in the story helped you to choose that word?

___

___

___

6 There was lots of fireweed at the cottage. Colour the arrow of the best answer.

a) The Kents were trying to grow more fireweed.

b) The Kents would like to get rid of the fireweed.

c) Fireweed is a fussy plant which is hard to grow.

7 What do you think Mr Kent wanted the goats to do around the cottage? Tick the correct answer.

a) Mr Kent wanted the goats to protect the cottage. ☐

b) Mr Kent wanted the goats to play with the green frogs. ☐

c) Mr Kent hoped the goats would eat the weeds and grass. ☐

TARGETING COMPREHENSION 4 © PASCAL PRESS ISBN 9781925490633

INFERRING

Would you like to go for a swim — inside a whale? The blue whale is so gigantic its heart is the size of a small car. You could even swim through its blood vessels! A fully grown blue whale is the largest mammal that's ever lived, and can weigh as much as 33 elephants. The blue whale is bigger than the biggest dinosaur. Now that's something to sing about!

Source: *That's Bizarre*, Pascal Press.

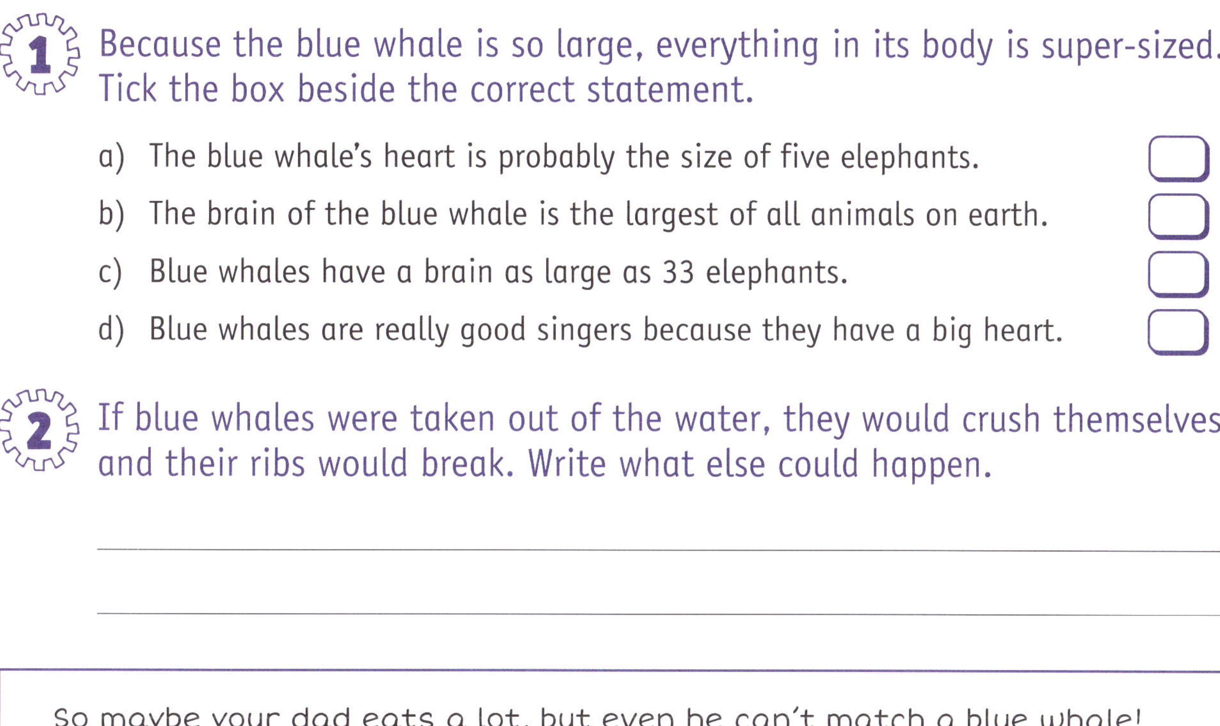

1 Because the blue whale is so large, everything in its body is super-sized. Tick the box beside the correct statement.

a) The blue whale's heart is probably the size of five elephants. ☐

b) The brain of the blue whale is the largest of all animals on earth. ☐

c) Blue whales have a brain as large as 33 elephants. ☐

d) Blue whales are really good singers because they have a big heart. ☐

2 If blue whales were taken out of the water, they would crush themselves and their ribs would break. Write what else could happen.

____

____

So maybe your dad eats a lot, but even he can't match a blue whale! These massive beasts eat small crustaceans called krill. They eat a few tonnes of krill every day.

Source: *That's Bizarre*, Pascal Press. [abridged]

3 Read the text above and colour the heart beside the correct statement.

a) Blue whales don't really eat very much.

b) Whales eat the weight of three small family cars each day.

c) Blue whales eat the weight of three children every day.

INFERRING

Imagine giving birth to 3000 babies every day! That's just what the termite queen does. This giant, fat white blob produces (makes) thousands of babies deep inside the termite mound where she lives for 20–50 years. Luckily, this monstrous mother has thousands of smaller termites ...

Source: *That's Bizarre*, Pascal Press. [abridged]

4 The queen termite does not have legs. What are some of the things that those thousands of termites might do for her and the mound?

____

____

____

____

5 Colour the shapes beside two statements that you think are correct.

a) Being so large, the queen needs to be fed by the termites. △

b) Building mounds is the job of the queen. □

c) The queen lives a lot longer than her babies. ◇

d) The queen cooks dinner for all the termites. ○

Shiver me timbers! Sea legends (stories) describe a massive sea monster called Kraken, which would attack ships with its long ________. Sailors thought this was just a story — until scientists discovered a giant squid as long as a bus living deep in the ocean. That's some colossal calamari!

Source: *That's Bizarre*, Pascal Press. [abridged]

6 What do you think the squid used to attack boats?

____

____

____

TARGETING COMPREHENSION 4 © PASCAL PRESS ISBN 9781925490633

INFERRING

Read this persuasive text and think about its main point.

DON'T KILL WASPS!

Wasps might seem like nasty insects because they sting, but they are actually our friends. They are a huge help to us because they kill insects which harm our food. People often kill them with insect spray which is harmful to them and our planet. Useful insects shouldn't be killed! We need them and so does our planet!

1 Read the following statements. Tick the box beside the one which is the best main idea for the text.

a) Wasps are annoying insects which should be sprayed and killed because they sting. ☐

b) Wasps are helpful insects because they fly a long way to sting us. ☐

c) Some insects are dangerous, you wouldn't want one to kill a friend. ☐

d) Some insects are helpful because they help to get rid of insects which destroy our food. ☐

Caterpillars eat and destroy food plants like tomatoes. However, as the caterpillars eat the tomato plant, the plant sends out an odour (smell) that acts like a message. When the wasp smells this, it comes flying. The wasp zeroes in and lands on the caterpillar. The wasp lays its eggs inside the caterpillar on the plant, and when they hatch, the baby wasps eat the caterpillar from the inside out.

Source: Brainwaves, *Plants That Bite Back*, Blake Education.

2 Read the information text above. What would you tell someone who is about to hurt a wasp that kills caterpillars?

____

____

____

The persuasive text shares some main points with the information text. Shade the sentences below which are common main points.

Information Text	a) Wasps are dangerous creatures that can give a nasty sting.
	b) There are some insects that are good to have around even though they sting.
	c) People who grow tomatoes should be happy to have wasps in their garden.
Persuasive Text	d) People who don't like insects are silly.
	e) Some insects can be used to get rid of other insects that harm our food.
	f) Tomatoes taste like rubbish and some insects kill them. That's good.

Spiders are not insects, but they do help us a lot with those pesky critters. Spiders eat heaps of insects. If they suddenly gave up eating insects, we could find ourselves knee-deep in those six-legged beasties!

Read the text about spiders. Colour the block beside the statement which is the best main idea for the text.

a) Spiders sometimes eat fruit. ☐

b) Spiders are not really going to give up eating insects. ☐

c) Spiders are creatures we can't do without. They help to control pests. ☐

d) Spiders should stop eating so many insects. ☐

e) Spiders are creepy and should be killed on sight. ☐

TARGETING COMPREHENSION 4 © PASCAL PRESS ISBN 9781925490633

Quick Guide to:

PREDICTING

Stone fish live on the bottom of reefs in the north of Australia. They don't move around much, lying amongst rocks and sand on the sea floor. They wait for dinner to just swim on by. Having long spines saves stone fish from being on the favourite food list of every creature in the ocean, as well as fishermen. The pain of a sting from these fish is said to drive humans crazy.

Tina's mum had told her about these terrible fish and she always wore shoes in shallow water. The fisherman who had just come to the beach walked straight into the water with nothing on his feet.

Answering questions about text often means finding the answer in what you have read. Sometimes you are asked to remember what was in the text. These are **literal** questions.

Example of a literal question:
Stone fish lie on the ocean floor. Where do stone fish live in Australia?

Answer: Stone fish are found in the north of Australia.

Unlike literal questions, when you **predict**, the answer is not in the text. **Predicting** is guessing what happens next or may happen in the text using what you have already read and understood.

Example of a predicting question:
Predict what may happen next to the man in the story.

Answer: The man who has bare feet may step on a stone fish and need to go to hospital.

DID YOU NOTICE?

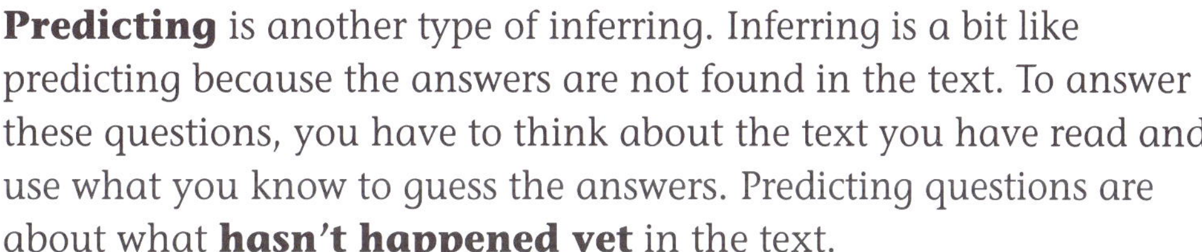

Predicting is another type of inferring. Inferring is a bit like predicting because the answers are not found in the text. To answer these questions, you have to think about the text you have read and use what you know to guess the answers. Predicting questions are about what **hasn't happened yet** in the text.

"There's no milk!" said Mum as she slammed the fridge door closed. She turned around and glared at me.

Luckily for me, the kitchen was full of patty cakes, cheese and biscuits, bowls of chips, sausage rolls, pickled onions, streamers, hats and blowers. In the middle of this there was a huge cake.

Luckily for me, Mum couldn't see the empty milk carton I'd just been drinking from. "They'll be here any minute. And he'll want a cup of tea," said Mum.

He was Grandpa, who drank twenty cups of tea a day. He used the same tea bag which he lugged around all day in a little green tin in his pocket. Disgusting!

Source: Sparklers, *Chocolate Chuckles*, Blake Education. [abridged]

1 The statements below predict what Mum might do next. Tick the box beside the one that you think is most likely.

Mum will ...

a) make some milk using milk powder and water. ☐

b) ask one of her neighbours for some milk. ☐

c) go to a nearby shop and buy milk. ☐

d) serve tea without milk. ☐

2 Can you guess what Mum is getting ready for? What are some of the words in the text that made you think this?

____

____

____

____

____

TARGETING COMPREHENSION 4 © PASCAL PRESS ISBN 9781925490633

PREDICTING

"You stay here, Sally, in case they arrive early. And don't touch anything. Promise?"

Me? Touch anything? Sometimes Mum sounded like she didn't trust me. I didn't touch anything. Except one patty cake and one chip — but they didn't really count.

Something was missing from the party food and I didn't mean the patty cake and the chip. Then it came to me — there were no chocolate crackles! I bolted across to the pantry and pulled the door open.

(*15 minutes later*) I heard Mum pull up in the drive. Another car pulled up straight behind her, so I had no time to ...

Source: Sparklers, *Chocolate Chuckles*, Blake Education. [abridged]

3 The statements below predict what happened when Sally realised there were no chocolate crackles. Colour the face of the one most likely.

a) Sally decided that no-one would like chocolate crackles anyway.	☺
b) Sally decided that she would go to the shop and buy chocolate crackles.	☺
c) Sally decided they must have chocolate crackles, so she would make some.	☺

4 What do you think Sally had no time to do before her mother arrived home?

____

____

____

5 Who do you think may have been in the car behind Sally's mum? Shade the sentence ending that has the best prediction.

The car behind Sally's mum was ...	a) the police because Sally's mum had been speeding.
	b) a guest who had arrived for the party.
	c) the neighbours who wanted to borrow some sugar.

PREDICTING

Some of the most extreme conditions (dangerous places) on Earth are found deep under the ocean. Fur seals withstand underwater pressure (weight) by collapsing their lungs and dropping their heart rate very low when they dive — sometimes as low as four beats per minute! Thankfully, humans invented (made) scuba tanks so we don't have to do this!

Source: *That's Bizarre*, Pascal Press. [abridged]

1 Fur seals have amazing abilities underwater. How does this help them? Tick any that apply.

They can ...

a) dive deep down into the sea. ☐

b) see well in the dark. ☐

c) hold their breath for a long time. ☐

d) have lots of fun. ☐

2 As humans, we cannot lower our heart rate very much. If we could, predict what we may be able to do when diving.

____

____

____

3 What would happen to submarines if they were not made of very strong steel? Shade the torpedo which answers this question.

TARGETING COMPREHENSION 4 © PASCAL PRESS ISBN 9781925490633

What do you think would win a deep diving contest — a submarine or a seal? Southern elephant seals can dive for two hours to depths of 1.7 kilometres, using just one breath. Humans can only dive to 180 metres, and even reinforced (thick metal) submarines have difficulty reaching the same depth as seals.

Source: *That's Bizarre*, Pascal Press. [abridged]

PREDICTING

4 Why do you think Southern elephant seals dive down so far into the water?

____

____

____

5 What might happen to a submarine that dived as far down as an elephant seal? Colour the box beside the correct answer.

a) It could get lost in the dark. ☐

b) It could scare the fish away. ☐

c) It could be damaged by an elephant seal. ☐

d) It could be crushed by the weight of the water. ☐

Humans have scuba tanks that allow them to breathe under water.

6 What do you predict would happen to a diver if they ever tried to swim down to 1.7 kilometres even with a scuba tank?

____

____

____

PREDICTING

Bikes are a great way to get about and a great way to exercise. They are cheap to run and easy to park. You can ride to school, roll through the park, or speed down the highway with the wind in your hair. You could compete in speed races, obstacle races, or cross-country time trials. Perhaps one day, you could even compete in Australia's *Tour Down Under*.

But ... like all people sharing the streets and roads ... there are rules!

You must wear a helmet. Your bike must have good brakes, and be fitted with a light, a bell and reflectors. In the city, you must ride in the designated bike lane — NOT on the footpath.

So, grab your water bottle and sweater, and come join the millions who enjoy bike riding every day.

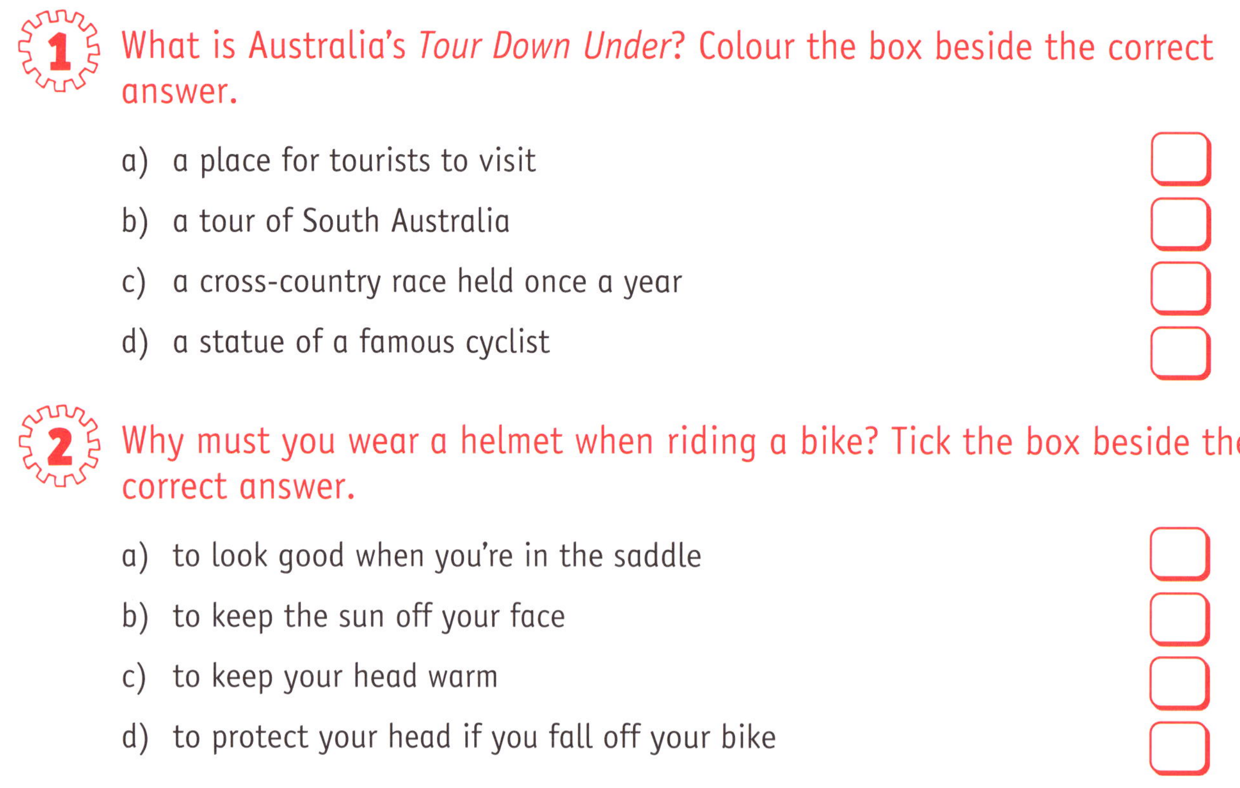

1 What is Australia's *Tour Down Under*? Colour the box beside the correct answer.

a) a place for tourists to visit

b) a tour of South Australia

c) a cross-country race held once a year

d) a statue of a famous cyclist

2 Why must you wear a helmet when riding a bike? Tick the box beside the correct answer.

a) to look good when you're in the saddle

b) to keep the sun off your face

c) to keep your head warm

d) to protect your head if you fall off your bike

TARGETING COMPREHENSION 4 © PASCAL PRESS ISBN 9781925490633

PREDICTING

3 Why should your bike have a light and reflectors? Tick the box of any that apply.

a) so you can ride fast at night ☐

b) so you can see where you're going after dark ☐

c) so you can read the names of the streets ☐

d) so other road users can see you at night ☐

4 Write one or two sentences to say why you should not ride on the footpath.

____

____

____

____

5 Why must your bike have a bell? Colour the box beside the correct answer.

a) to annoy other road users ☐

b) to greet your friends as you ride by ☐

c) to warn people that you are behind them ☐

d) to scare dogs away ☐

Quick Guide to:

ANALYSING

Humans are dopey creatures. They think that they own the planet or something. This is really silly because everyone in the ocean knows that the owners are the whales and dolphins.

Whales and dolphins are never going to destroy the oceans and all the creatures in them. They have too much respect for that to happen. Whales know that without clean oceans the world may be in very big trouble.

Humans throw rubbish into the water, hunt and kill too many fish, and spread their poisons everywhere. Humans, dolphins and whales need clean air to survive, but even this is being messed up. Sea plants and creatures are slowly starting to die and this may be what happens to all creatures on Earth.

Answering questions about text often means finding the answer in what you have read. Sometimes you are asked to remember what was in the text. These are **literal** questions.

Example of a literal question:
What is one way humans are putting our sea creatures in danger?

Answer: Humans are putting rubbish into the ocean and this is poisoning the water.

Unlike literal questions, when you **analyse**, the answer is not in the text. **Analysing** is reading and thinking about all the information and guessing what idea this is giving to readers.

Example of an analysing question:
What is the difference between whales, dolphins and humans in the way they treat the oceans?

Answer: Whales and dolphins respect the oceans but humans don't care and may end up destroying all life.

DID YOU NOTICE?

When you **analyse** text, you have to read carefully and use the information to make up your mind about **what is really meant**. When you infer and predict, you also have to do this. Analysing means that all of the text needs to be thought about.

TARGETING COMPREHENSION 4 © PASCAL PRESS ISBN 9781925490633

Imaginative Text

Three children were waiting for her. The boy in the group was none other than Ronald Higgins. Last year, Ronald had laughed loudly when one of the boys fell off a pony and landed in a patch of thistles (prickles). Emma couldn't stand him.

Source: Giggler*s*, *Sneeze Power*, Blake Education.

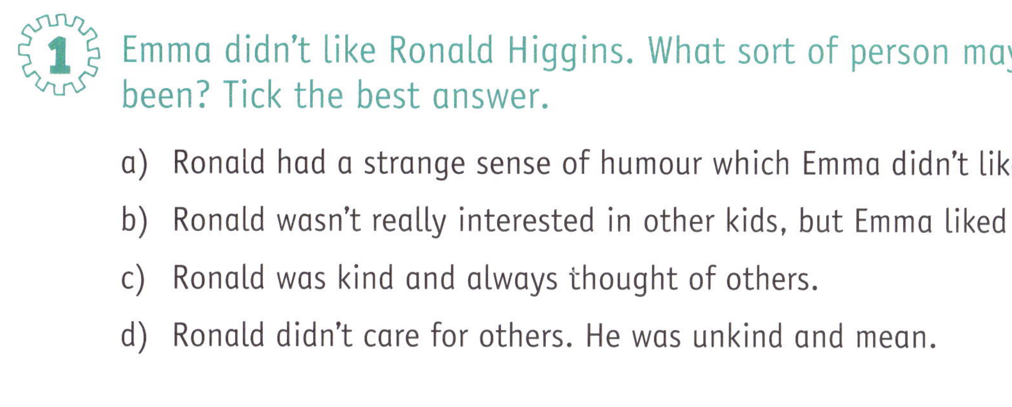

1 Emma didn't like Ronald Higgins. What sort of person may Ronald have been? Tick the best answer.

a) Ronald had a strange sense of humour which Emma didn't like. ☐

b) Ronald wasn't really interested in other kids, but Emma liked him. ☐

c) Ronald was kind and always thought of others. ☐

d) Ronald didn't care for others. He was unkind and mean. ☐

ANALYSING

2 If adults had been watching when the boy fell off the pony, what would they think of Ronald? What might they say to him?

____

____

____

____

Ronald's father strode up. "Why is my boy riding that ridiculous pony?" he demanded. He was so angry that you could see his tonsils when he shouted. "He should change places with that girl." He jabbed his finger in Emma's direction.

Source: Gigglers, *Sneeze Power*, Blake Education.

If you were going to tell someone about Ronald's father, you might use some of the words below.

thoughtful	rude	selfish	mean
friendly	pleasant	nice	kind

Write a sentence about Ronald's father using some of the words.

____

____

____

Ronald made a big deal out of scooping up some chaff (straw) and putting it into the feed trough. "Thank you, Ronald. Well done," said Ms Kate. Ronald smirked at Emma. He mouthed the word "carrot-top". Suddenly, a loud sneeze exploded in the barn. A bundle of straw swept up from the floor and landed in Ronald's mouth. All the children exploded with laughter, and Emma and Alice linked little fingers.

Source: Gigglers, *Sneeze Power*, Blake Education.

Ronald and Emma didn't get on. What sort of a person was Ronald? Draw a line from Ronald's name to the group of words that best tell about him.

thoughtful of animals and showed kindness

was a bully who enjoyed upsetting others

Ronald

just wanted to be friends with Emma

enjoyed being around Emma

Shade the statement below that you think tells how Ronald may have been feeling about being thanked.

Ronald only wanted to help out and was happy that he was able to do this.

Ronald thought that he was smart because he got away with his bad behaviour.

TARGETING COMPREHENSION 4 © PASCAL PRESS ISBN 9781925490633

Look out behind you! Crocodiles stalk their prey and are experts at creeping up behind their victims. They can move with surprising speed and agility. In their own environment, they are easily faster than humans! They have 64 large teeth that they use to crush small prey, swallowing it whole. But don't feel too secure. Larger prey is shaken to pieces first!

Source: *That's Lethal*, Pascal Press. [abridged]

ANALYSING

1 The writer is telling us something we should remember when in a crocodile environment. Tick the box of the best statement.

a) Crocodiles are dangerous creatures that move fast, so stay away! ☐

b) Crocodiles might be fast, but there's nothing to worry about really. ☐

c) In a crocodile's environment, listen carefully and you'll be safe. ☐

d) Crocodiles have so many teeth they are not able to attack humans. ☐

2 What advice would you give to a person who has no idea about crocodiles?

____

____

____

3 There are signs about crocodiles around creeks and on beaches warning of the danger. Colour the sign which best tells about crocodile danger.

THERE ARE CROCODILES HERE!

STAY CLEAR! Crocodiles are fast and dangerous!

DANGER! Crocodiles are Swift and Silent Killers!

What looks like a sunken branch and has eyes, ears and a nose? If you don't know the answer, you're in trouble! When hunting, crocodiles hide in shallow water with only their nostrils, ears and eyes poking out. This allows them to detect approaching prey while remaining hidden. Crocs can look like bits of rotting timber — until they suddenly launch themselves at lunch. They can rush several metres to snap at prey. Pray that it isn't you.

Source: *That's Lethal*, Pascal Press. [abridged]

ANALYSING

4 Read the text about the danger of crocodiles. Write down two ways they are dangerous to people.

____

____

____

5 We could be in trouble if we don't know how crocodiles are dangerous. Colour any statements below that explain why crocodiles are a danger.

a) Crocodiles aren't dangerous animals. You can get close enough to see their eyes and nose. △

b) Beware of any floating timber in crocodile territory because it may be a croc. □

c) Crocodiles hunt their prey by having their nose and eyes out of the water. Watch out for these. ◇

d) Crocodiles like to spend time having most of their body covered by water. ○

6 The writer is telling us about the danger of crocodiles. How can you stay safe in crocodile territory?

____

____

____

TARGETING COMPREHENSION 4 © PASCAL PRESS ISBN 9781925490633

Targeting Comprehension

Year 4 Answers

Literal

Page 2

1 True
2 d
3 ***Sample answer*** Franklin was upset because he had lost/couldn't find his friend.
4 b
5 couch, chair, chicken, sink, friend
6 c
7 happy, joyful, glad
8 True

Page 4

1 worn, moved
2 b
3 physical erosion
4 ***Sample answer*** A flood could cause erosion by carrying away bits of soil and sand.
5 True
6 answers will vary

Page 6

1 b
2 ***Sample answer*** Soccer is good for your heart because you usually run a lot when you play soccer and running is good for your heart.
3 True
4 spending time together; enjoying the same activities
5 playing, sitting, running, dribbling, passing
6 dribbling a ball, passing a ball, shielding the ball, tackling players, kicking goals
7 get fit; make friends; learn new skills

Inferring

Page 9

1 c
2 ***Sample answer*** The Kents may have used the water in the dam for drinking, washing and watering the garden.
3 b (best answer)
4 tools, lawn mower, old bikes, garden tools
5 answers will vary
6 b
7 c

Page 11

1 b
2 ***Sample answer*** They would die. / They wouldn't be able to breathe. / Their body, lungs and heart would be crushed.
3 b
4 ***Sample answer*** The termites bring her food and water, and they protect her.
5 a, c
6 ***Sample answer*** The squid probably used its tentacles or beak.

Page 13

1 d
2 ***Sample answer*** Don't hurt wasps because they are helpful to us by killing caterpillars.
3 b, e
4 c

Predicting

Page 16

1 c
2 ***Sample answer*** Mum is getting ready for a party because there are streamers, hats, blowers, a cake and party food.
3 c
4 ***Sample answer*** Sally probably didn't have time to finish making the chocolate crackles and clean up.
5 b

Page 18

1 a, c
2 ***Sample answer*** Humans might be able to dive deeper and hold our breath for longer.
3 They would be crushed.
4 ***Sample answer*** The Southern elephant seals dive deep to find food.
5 d
6 ***Sample answer*** They would be crushed by the water pressure and die.

Page 20

1 c
2 d
3 b, d
4 answers will vary
5 c

Analysing

Page 23

1 d
2 ***Sample answer*** Adults would think Ronald was rude and nasty. They might tell him to apologise for laughing.
3 Answers will vary using the words: rude, selfish and mean in a sentence.
4 was a bully who enjoyed upsetting others
5 Ronald thought that he was smart because he got away with his behaviour.

Page 25

1 a
2 ***Sample answer*** Be careful, crocodiles are fast and dangerous, and can sneak up on you.
3 DANGER! Crocodiles are Swift and Silent Killers!
4 ***Sample answer*** Crocodiles hide well and can't be seen, and they're very fast.
5 b, c, d
6 ***Sample answer*** Stay away from creeks and beaches in crocodile territory. Take care and only walk and swim in safe areas.

Page 27

1 c
2 answers will vary
3 a – good, b – bad, c – bad, d – good, e – bad
4 ***Sample answer*** Chocolate makers might be unhappy about the information in this text because they won't sell as much chocolate.
5 TOO MUCH CHOCOLATE IS BAD FOR YOUR HEALTH!

TARGETING COMPREHENSION 4 © PASCAL PRESS ISBN 9781925490633

Making Connections

Page 30

1 c
2 ***Sample answer*** Tessa was interested in Gran's story as she looked at her eagerly.
3 a
4 Tessa circled the date on the calendar that Gran's friend was coming to visit.
5 c
6 b

Page 32

1 d
2 ***Sample answer*** The sea tulip would die as it needs to live in the sea with salty sea water.
3 a
4 ***Sample answer*** Cherry tomatoes are small and don't weigh much — just like a koala's brain.
5 ***Sample answer*** Koalas have a small brain and are not very smart.
6 Elephant seals are about the same size as a big bus.

Page 34

1 b
2 cool nerves, courage, talent, skill, brave
3 answers will vary
4 If the skiers crashed into the trees and rocks, they could die from the impact.
5 Downhill skiing is a crazy, amazing sport. (persuasive text coloured yellow)
It takes courage and good safety gear to be a speed skier. (information text coloured blue)
6 1: It takes cool nerves and top-notch protection (safety gear) to be a speed skier.
2: You'd have to have so much courage, talent and skill.

Critical Reflection

Page 37

1 b
2 ***Sample answer*** Todd was thinking that they would get in trouble from Mr Lewis for being out of class.
3 c
4 ***Sample answer*** He won't really die, but he is extremely bored.
5 d
6 ***Sample answer*** Mr Lewis was probably feeling happy and clever that he had caught the boys out of class.

Page 39

1 a – 4, b – 1, c – 2, d – 3
2 ***Sample answers***
Step 2: I would ring an ambulance.
Step 3: I would stay calm and sit still.
3 a, b
4 ***Sample answer*** Check the mouse cage for spiders and webs, and keep the cage indoors.
5 b, c, d

Page 41

1 d
2 a, c, d
3 ***Sample answer*** The writer uses the fear of darkness to engage the reader. Some words, such as dark, scary and deadly, are capitalised to stand out.
4 b, c, d
5 b

Assessment

Page 43

1 frog
2 a – 3, b – 2, c – 1, d – 4
3 True
4 Tadpoles have gills so they can breathe under water.
5 front legs grow; tail begins to get shorter; hop out of the water
6 swimming, eating, grow, breathe, hop, lay
7 insects

Page 45

1 a smile, some courage, yourself!
2 That's OK
3 No
4 To find out more about them and see if you have things in common.
5 lunch, books, sport, superheroes, movies, TV shows
6 listen, wait, talk
7 True

Page 47

1 d
2 c
3 a
4 Bushfires Kill! Do NOT Light Fires!
5 ***Sample answer*** People would take notice of this sign because of the word 'kill'.
6 b

Page 49

1 ***Sample answer*** We should protect our oceans so that sea animals don't die and our environment is clean. Sea animals are a source of food for us too.
2 BANS IMPOSED ON DUMPING CHEMICALS DOWN DRAINS
3 c
4 Having so many things on her bike, she fell off at the bottom of the hill.
5 They add colour and flavour, and have health benefits.

Page 51

1 ***Sample answer*** What we do on land affects sea creatures, so we need to dispose of rubbish correctly. Otherwise, whales and other sea animals may become extinct.
2 The writer wanted readers to know that it is stupid to light fires in summer that could cause bushfires, threatening people, homes and property.
3 d
4 Milly would have been seen as a bully by other students.

Page 53

1 a
2 c
3 d
4 Curved claws …

Page 55

1 ***Sample answer*** People could store water and food, have torches ready, and secure and tie down things outside.
2 ***Sample answer*** Cyclones are dangerous and because they don't come every day, they need to be planned for.
3 ***Sample answer*** The booklet gave the wrong information so she was in danger of a bear attack because of what she read.
4 d
5 b

TARGETING COMPREHENSION 4 © PASCAL PRESS ISBN 9781925490633

Chocolate is really bad for you and you should give it up as soon as you can. Full of fat, this sweet can make you the same way — FULL OF FAT! Chocolate is also full of sugar. Sugar is the dentist's friend! All those amazing holes in your teeth will keep your dentist busy for years. Who would choose to have holes in their teeth big enough to need fillings made in a cement mixer?

ANALYSING

What are the choices the writer is giving you? Tick the box which best says the choices being given.

The writer is saying ...

a) eat chocolate and help dentists make more money. ☐

b) eat chocolate and have your teeth cleaned more. ☐

c) eat chocolate and you'll be unhealthy in two different ways. ☐

d) eat chocolate and get really fat, but be very, very happy. ☐

Here are some results of research into chocolate.

1) Dark chocolate may protect your skin from the sun.
2) The sugar in chocolate gives us energy and relaxes the body.
3) Chocolate may improve our heart health.
4) Dark chocolate could improve memory.

Consider the good and bad points about chocolate and write about what is important to you when choosing to eat chocolate.

ANALYSING

3 Read each fact about chocolate below. Colour a box to show whether chocolate is good for your health or bad for your health.

	Good	Bad
a) Chocolate has been found by doctors to improve mood (make you feel better).	☐	☐
b) Chocolate is full of fat. Eating too much chocolate can cause health problems.	☐	☐
c) Chocolate has lots of sugar.	☐	☐
d) Chocolate gives lots of energy quickly. Soldiers carry chocolate in their kit bags for this reason.	☐	☐
e) Because chocolate has lots of sugar, eating it may lead to tooth decay.	☐	☐

4 Who would be unhappy about what is said in this text? Give reasons for your answer.

____

____

____

5 Newspapers and TV use headlines to catch our attention. Shade one block for the headline that goes best with the text.

HEADLINE	Blocks
CHOCOLATE IS GREAT FOR YOU — EAT MORE!	
TOO MUCH CHOCOLATE IS BAD FOR YOUR HEALTH!	
EATING TOO MUCH CHOCOLATE CAN BE DANGEROUS!	
THE EASTER BUNNY MAY BE A DANGEROUS KILLER!	
YOU CAN'T EAT TOO MUCH CHOCOLATE!	

TARGETING COMPREHENSION 4 © PASCAL PRESS ISBN 9781925490633

Quick Guide to:

MAKING CONNECTIONS

There is an old joke that says, "A sea turtle is so slow it gets lost going around in a circle". This could be true because they really are that slow.

For a really boring creature which everyone thought was not all that brainy, Ted was really quite a good thinker. He was the only turtle in the sea that worried about the number of small turtles that weren't showing up out in the ocean after the hatching season.

Ted had watched the sea birds, lizards and humans steal from the nests made by mother turtles. He had tried to tell all the other turtles and sea creatures about this, but they kept falling asleep and snoring so loudly that they never actually heard what he was saying.

Answering questions about text often means finding the answer in what you have read. Sometimes you are asked to remember what was in the text. These are **literal** questions.

Example of a literal question:
What happened when Ted tried to tell the other turtles about the stolen eggs?

Answer: They kept falling asleep and didn't hear what he was saying.

Making connections starts with reading and thinking about all the text. These questions ask you to think about why things in the text are linked or have an effect on another piece of text. **Making connections** asks you to think how two or more different things or actions affect each other.

Example of a making connections question:
Why was the number of small turtles decreasing?

Answer: Sea birds, lizards and humans were stealing the eggs, so the turtles weren't being hatched.

DID YOU NOTICE?

Making connections means thinking about two things in the story and working out **how these are linked** or connected. In the answer above, the sea turtle wasn't listened to or thought of as a good thinker. This happens because he was slow and the other turtles and sea creatures went to sleep. This is not because of what he had to say.

Tessa's Great Gran had just received a letter from her friend Amelia in America.

"Gadzooks and gadzillion," groaned Great Gran. "I haven't seen Amelia for fifty years. Not since we were young women. She was such a beauty. All the young men adored her. They would line up from her dad's farm to the rabbit-proof fence for one of her smiles."

Tessa could see a story coming. She perched on the fence, her eyes began shining eagerly. "And?"

It was all Great Gran needed to get her started. "Amelia could have chosen any one of the boys but she fell in love with an American sailor we met at the Christmas Eve dance. They were married just four weeks later because he had to go to sea. A few days later, I went to the harbour to say goodbye to them."

Source: Gigglers, *Getting Rid of Wrinkles*, Blake Education. [abridged]

MAKING CONNECTIONS

1 How do you think Great Gran was feeling after getting the letter? Tick the best statement.

a) Great Gran was happy to hear from her old friend. ☐

b) Great Gran wasn't really interested and put the letter in the bin. ☐

c) Great Gran was feeling surprised and a bit nervous. ☐

d) Great Gran was very worried about her friend. ☐

2 How do you think Tessa was feeling about Great Gran's story? Write your answer in a sentence and give a reason.

____

____

____

3 What happened after Amelia got married? Tick the box that shows what most likely happened.

a) Amelia left by ship to live in America with her husband. ☐

b) Amelia sailed to New Zealand with her husband. ☐

c) Amelia took a plane to America and her husband went by ship. ☐

TARGETING COMPREHENSION 4 © PASCAL PRESS ISBN 9781925490633

Great Gran checked the letter again. "Of course I am pleased. But what will I do? I can't let her see me like this. I've got just ten days to get rid of my wrinkles."

Tessa bounced down off the fence, "Don't worry, I'll help." They hurried indoors. Great Gran let Tessa draw a big circle around a date on the calendar.

Source: Gigglers, *Getting Rid of Wrinkles*, Blake Education. [abridged]

Why do you think Tessa marked a date on the calendar with a large circle?

____

____

"I've got an idea," said Tessa. "If you stand on your head, you might unwrinkle, like when Mum hangs creased clothes on a hanger."

"That may work. But it's been such a long time since I did anything like that. You'd better catch my legs," said Great Gran.

Source: Gigglers, *Getting Rid of Wrinkles*, Blake Education.

Colour the block of the statement which best tells what happened next in the story.

a) Tessa was only joking and Great Gran baked a cake. ☐

b) Great Gran was very fit and stood on her head for hours. ☐

c) Being old, Great Gran fell over and got a headache. ☐

d) Great Gran's wrinkles started to disappear. ☐

That gave Tessa time to think. "Steam," she said at last. "That gets the crinkles out really well when Mum's doing the ironing."

Source: Gigglers, *Getting Rid of Wrinkles*, Blake Education.

Shade the box that tells what might happen next in the story.

a) Tessa tried to iron her grandmother's face.
b) Tessa asked her grandmother to put a towel over her head near a bowl of steaming water.
c) Tessa rang her mum about ironing.
d) Tessa put hot water over her grandmother's face.

Sea tulips may sound like flowers, but forget about putting them in vases! They are a type of sea squirt. They cling to rocks or coral their whole lives and they don't move. Many people throughout the world regard them as delicacies (rare and tasty food).

Source: *That's Bizarre*, Pascal Press.

1 Why do you think some sea squirts are called sea 'tulips'?

a) They live in the sea. ☐
b) They suck food out of sea water. ☐
c) They grow on a rock. ☐
d) They look like flowers with long stalks. ☐

2 Sea tulips are sea creatures. What do you think would happen if you put one in a vase of fresh water? Explain your answer.

____

____

____

The pineapple fish is yellow and spiny just like a real pineapple! But don't try to eat this one. When they feel threatened (scared), they use spines in their fins to protect themselves. Not-so-smoothie!

Source: *That's Bizarre*, Pascal Press.

3 The writer is comparing a fish with a fruit. Read the statements below and shade three faces of the one that is totally right.

Statement	
a) Pineapples are like this fish because they are yellow, spiny and a little round.	
b) Because pineapples are able to be eaten, they are like this fish.	
c) Pineapples make great smoothies but have spines just like this fish.	

TARGETING COMPREHENSION 4 © PASCAL PRESS ISBN 9781925490633

Koalas have teensy-weensy brains. Their brain weighs 17 grams, which is about the size of a cherry tomato. Don't ask them to do long division!

Source: *That's Bizarre*, Pascal Press.

4 The writer is comparing a koala brain with a cherry tomato. How are they the same?

____

____

____

____

5 Why do you think that the writer says, 'Don't ask them to do long division'?

____

____

____

A male elephant seal can weigh up to 3700 kilograms! With a length of up to 5 metres, that makes them bigger than a ________. Five metres is about the same length as a large room in your home.

Source: *That's Bizarre*, Pascal Press. [abridged]

6 Below are four statements that tell us how big an elephant seal may be. Shade the statement that is most accurate.

Elephant seals are …

- … about the same size as a big bus.
- … about the same length and weight as a car.
- … about the size and weight as the classroom.
- … about the same size as a house.

MAKING CONNECTIONS

Would you plunge down the side of a mountain on a pair of skis at speeds of 240 kilometres per hour? It takes cool nerves and top-notch protection (safety gear) to be a speed skier. Rocks, boulders and trees can be deadly and helmets are essential (really needed).

Source: Brainwaves, *To the Limit*, Blake Education. [abridged]

Read both texts. They give similar information but the text below is written persuasively.

Plunging down a steep and dangerous slope at a million kilometres an hour — how crazy is that? You'd have to have so much courage, talent and skill. Downhill skiers are crazy, brave superstars with a huge death wish. Guts of that type are rare. This is when a tree or a rock can be your worst enemy. You need radical equipment that could save your life! This sport is cool to the max!

MAKING CONNECTIONS

1 Why does the writer say downhill skiers are 'crazy'? Tick your answer.

a) They wear helmets. ☐

b) They ski down steep slopes at great speed. ☐

c) They like winter sports. ☐

d) They have great skill and good protection. ☐

2 List words or phrases from both texts that show the qualities of a downhill skier.

3 How would you answer the question in the first text — Would you plunge down the side of a mountain on a pair of skis at speeds of 240 kilometres per hour? Give your reasons.

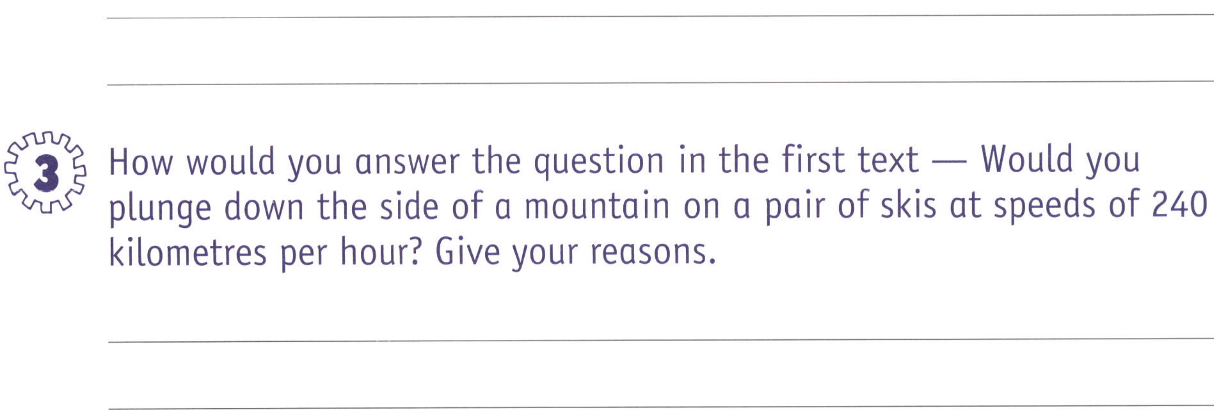

TARGETING COMPREHENSION 4 © PASCAL PRESS ISBN 9781925490633

4 Why do the writers of both texts say that trees and rocks can be deadly?

____

____

____

____

5 Both texts have a main idea. Colour the main idea of the **information text blue** and the main idea of the **persuasive text yellow**.

- Downhill skiing is a crazy, amazing sport.

- It takes courage and good safety gear to be a speed skier.

6 Find a sentence in the first text that has the same meaning as a sentence from the second text. The words will be different, but their meaning will be the same. Write them below.

1. ____

____

2. ____

____

MAKING CONNECTIONS

Quick Guide to:

• CRITICAL REFLECTION •

Humans throw plenty of rubbish into the water, but blue plastic strapping from bait boxes is the worst. These are circles of death which dolphins and other sea animals think are playthings. Made of tough plastic, these strangle or cut to the bone once around the animal. Creatures suffer an agonising death.

Roger the crocodile had become a hero. Yes, this scaly, toothy and evil-looking creature was famous amongst sea creatures. Roger had learned to chase any sea creature he saw caught in a blue strap. Swimming up behind them, he'd snap the plastic with his powerful jaws. Animals who hadn't heard about Roger were more than worried when he swam toward them ...

Answering questions about text often means finding the answer in what you have read. Sometimes you are asked to remember what was in the text. These are **literal** questions.

Example of a literal question:
What did Roger do to help other sea creatures?

Answer: Roger would help animals by chasing them and biting through the plastic straps.

Critical reflection starts with reading and thinking about all the text. These questions ask you to think about how things happen, how they affect what is happening and the feelings of characters.

Example of a critical reflection question:
Creatures who didn't know Roger were worried when he swam towards them. What were they thinking and how would they have felt after being helped?

Answer: Because Roger was a crocodile, they would have been scared of being eaten. After they were helped, they would have been grateful.

DID YOU NOTICE?

The answer is not in the text. You have to **read and decide** how the characters are thinking. You have to read and think about your feelings about a character, or about a topic. You have to **use your ideas** to find the answer by thinking of your experiences.

TARGETING COMPREHENSION 4 © PASCAL PRESS ISBN 9781925490633

"Why aren't you two in class?" barked Mr Lewis from the teachers' staffroom doorway. Todd and Scott stopped in their tracks.

"Oh-oh," Todd said under his breath.

Source: Gigglers, *Hear Me Roar*, Blake Education.

1. Todd and Scott were stopped by their principal, Mr Lewis. Tick the box of the statement that best tells about what was happening.

   a) Todd and Scott were just on a message for their teacher. ☐
   b) Todd and Scott were not where they were supposed to be. ☐
   c) Todd and Scott were not really worried about seeing Mr Lewis. ☐
   d) Todd and Scott were going to the toilet and weren't worried. ☐

2. What do you think Todd was thinking when he said, "oh-oh"?

____

____

____

"I said, why aren't you two in class?" Mr Lewis repeated, edging nearer.

Todd's mind raced through a list of excuses, none of which sounded good enough. He knew Mr Lewis wouldn't understand just how dull maths with Miss Connor could be. He wouldn't understand the threat of dying of boredom, which Todd was positive really could happen.

Source: Gigglers, *Hear Me Roar*, Blake Education. [abridged]

3. Shade the shape next to the statement that says what Mr Lewis was probably thinking when he saw the boys.

   a) I think that these boys have been naughty and sent out of class. △
   b) I'll make sure that these boys know not to be out of class. □
   c) There is no reason for these boys being out of class. I'll find out why they are. ○

4 Todd thought that he may die of boredom. Does this mean that he would really die? What is Todd's problem?

____

____

____

Todd had dared Scott to slip out of class with him. No, Mr Lewis would not understand any of this. So he mumbled the excuse everybody uses in this kind of situation, "Toilet."

Well almost everyone. Unfortunately, Scott said the second most popular excuse at the same time, "Library."

A moment of awkward silence passed. Mr Lewis smirked victoriously, like a hunter who had just caught a prized prey, before finally saying, "Come with me."

Source: Gigglers, *Hear Me Roar*, Blake Education.

5 When the boys gave a different excuse at the same time, what would you infer (guess) that Mr Lewis was thinking? Tick the statement that is most likely.

a) These two boys are going to the toilet and then the library. ☐

b) I'll let these two go where they say they are going. ☐

c) I'm not sure, but these boys may be fibbing. ☐

d) These boys are telling fibs, they can't get their story right. ☐

6 'Like a hunter who had just caught a prized prey.' This is a simile which compares two different things. Describe in your own words how Mr Lewis was feeling about catching the boys out of class.

____

____

____

Spiders use fangs to catch their food. They bite down deep and then inject venom into the victim's wound. One type of venom paralyses, stopping the prey from escaping. Another type destroys tissue (flesh), causing festering ulcers (sores). Delicious rotting spider stew! Only about 30 spider species throughout the world are a threat to humans — um only?? Murder weapons aren't always left at the scene of the crime. Spiders take theirs with them!

Source: *That's Lethal*, Pascal Press. [abridged]

1 Read the sentences below, which tell you how spiders hunt and kill their prey. Number the boxes from 1 to 4 in the correct order of how they do this.

a) Spiders then stick their fangs into the victim and suck out their innards. ☐

b) Spiders trap their victims in their sticky webs. ☐

c) Spiders inject their venom (poison) into their victims. ☐

d) The venom then paralyses the victim. ☐

2 What do you think you would do if you were bitten by a venomous spider? Write two other steps in order. The first step is written for you.

Step 1 The first thing I would do if I was bitten, would be to tell Mum or Dad.

Step 2 ______________________________

____

____

____

Step 3 ______________________________

____

____

____

CRITICAL REFLECTION

3 Read the sentences below about spider venom. Tick two boxes that you think are correct.

a) Toxins (poisons) in the venom stop the brain working properly. ☐

b) The animal cannot move because the poison stops the brain from working. ☐

c) The venom of spiders such as funnel webs is not very poisonous. ☐

d) The victim isn't in that much danger. ☐

> Keep a close eye on your pet mice. Red-backs would like nothing more than to turn them into a tasty meal! These clever spiders are a dab hand (clever) at setting up snares. When an insect or animal strays into their web, the snare is released and the prey is hoisted off the ground.
>
> Source: *That's Lethal*, Pascal Press.

4 What would you suggest people do with their pet mice to stop spiders biting them?

____

____

____

____

5 **ADVICE:** Spider safety is important because a spider is never more than **15 metres away from you – EVER!** Read the advice and colour the stars that give good advice.

a) Watch for spiders! Pick them up with bare hands and throw them outside. 

b) Check around for spider webs each day.

c) Check outside and inside the house for spider webs. Do not touch them, tell an adult. 

d) Watch for spiders which may be under parts of the fence.

CRITICAL REFLECTION

TARGETING COMPREHENSION 4 © PASCAL PRESS ISBN 9781925490633

1st Caving (going into caves) takes us deep within the earth. Down there in the dark, it is a very different world to the one that we know. Caving involves crawling, squeezing, sliding and stooping, often in mud and water. Cavers just have to be sure they can find their way back up and out.

Source: Brainwaves, *To the Limit*, Blake Education. [abridged]

Read the text below. This gives the same information but has been written persuasively.

2nd Caving is not for the faint-hearted! It's a DARK and SCARY world down there below the surface of the earth. Imagine crawling through narrow tunnels and caves in the cold and silence, with just a headlamp to show the way! Imagine sloshing through the mud and water, and squeezing through narrow openings! YUK! It would be very easy to get lost. The DEADLY question is: How do you find your way back to the surface?

1 Why do you think people go caving? Colour the box beside your answer.

a) to look for buried treasure ☐
b) because they like dark, scary places ☐
c) to search for gold ☐
d) to explore the underground world ☐

2 In the second text, what does the writer want you to think about caving? Tick any answers that apply.

a) Caving requires a high level of fitness and courage. ☐
b) Caving is an amazing sport and lots of fun. ☐
c) Caving can be dangerous. ☐
d) Caving takes you into a cold, dark and silent world. ☐

CRITICAL REFLECTION

3 How does the writer of the 2nd text grab your attention?

4 What do you think is important if you are going caving? Colour any thought bubbles that apply.

a) Taking a mobile phone.

b) Taking plenty of water to drink.

c) Wearing warm clothes and sturdy walking shoes.

d) Telling someone where you are going.

5 Both texts tell of the risk of getting lost while caving. What do you think you should do if you were lost? Colour the box next to your answer.

a) Phone home and ask someone to help.

b) Stay where you are and wait for help to come.

c) Try to look for a way out.

d) Scream loudly, and hope someone hears you.

CRITICAL REFLECTION

TARGETING COMPREHENSION 4 © PASCAL PRESS ISBN 9781925490633

Literal

Frogs go through several stages of life before they become adults.

Frogs start their lives as a tiny clear egg with a black dot. Female frogs can lay hundreds of eggs at once. Once the eggs hatch, they become tadpoles.

Tadpoles look like little fish and they don't have any legs. They use gills to breathe under the water. Tadpoles spend their time swimming and eating plants. During this time, their back legs begin to grow and they begin to develop lungs so they can breathe out of the water.

As tadpoles start to become young frogs, their front legs begin to grow and their tail becomes shorter. Once their tails are almost gone, the tiny frogs will hop out of the water. The little frogs' tails eventually disappear and they start to eat insects instead of plants.

It can take 2–4 years for a frog to become an adult. The female frog can then lay her own eggs and the lifecycle starts all over again.

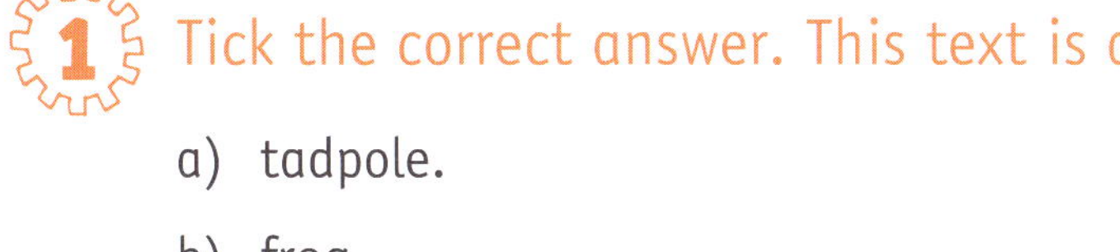

1 Tick the correct answer. This text is about the lifecycle of a ...

a) tadpole. ☐

b) frog. ☐

c) fish. ☐

d) egg. ☐

2 Number these stages of life in the correct order from 1 to 4.

a) young frog ☐

b) tadpole ☐

c) egg ☐

d) adult frog ☐

3 True or False? Female frogs can lay many eggs at once.

☐ True ☐ False

4 Why do tadpoles have gills?

____

____

5 What three important things happen as a tadpole becomes a young frog?

a) ______________________________

b) ______________________________

c) ______________________________

6 Circle the verbs (action words) used in the text.

swimming	chew	eating
jump	grow	run
breathe	hop	lay

7 What food do frogs eat?

____

ASSESSMENT

TARGETING COMPREHENSION 4 © PASCAL PRESS ISBN 9781925490633

How to Make a New Friend

Making new friends can be hard at first but you can make it easier by following the steps below. This is how you can make a new friend at lunchtime.

What you need:

- a smile
- some courage
- yourself!

What you can do:

1. Walk up to someone with a smile.
2. Notice if they look at you (give you eye contact) and smile back.
3. Ask if you can sit with them. If they say no, just say, "That's OK". You can be brave and ask someone else. If they say yes, say, "Thanks" and join them.
4. If you don't know each other's names, make sure you introduce yourself.
5. Try to find something in common by asking the other person questions. You could ask what they have for lunch; their favourite sport, movie or TV show; or even ask about their favourite book or superhero. This is a way you'll get to know them.
6. Listen to what the other person has to say and wait until it's your turn to talk.
7. Ask what they're planning to do during lunchtime and ask if you can join them.

These steps might not work every time and that's OK. The point is that you are being brave and kind, and doing your best to find a new friend. Make sure you do the same for others when they ask to join you. Include them as much as possible.

1 Name three things you need to make a friend.

a) ______________________________

b) ______________________________

c) ______________________________

ASSESSMENT

Literal

2 What can you say if someone says you can't sit with them?

____

3 Do you need to introduce yourself if you already know each other's names?

☐ Yes ☐ No

4 Why should you ask the other person some questions?

____

____

____

5 Circle the topics (nouns) mentioned in the text that you could talk about.

lunch	friends	school	books
teachers	sport	pets	superheroes
movies	family	TV shows	music

6 When talking, you should ______________ to what the other person has to say and ______________ until it's your turn to ______________.

7 True or False? Sometimes you have to be brave in order to make new friends.

☐ True ☐ False

ASSESSMENT

TARGETING COMPREHENSION 4 © PASCAL PRESS ISBN 9781925490633

Inferring

Thomas decided not to speak to his dad ever again. Not one word.

"I'll pick you up at four," said Dad. Thomas said nothing. "I'm sorry I can't come with you, Son. This meeting just came up."

"On our Saturday afternoon?" Thomas thought, but he kept his lips closed.

"I'll come next time," said his father. Thomas got out of the car.
"I promise," his dad called from the front seat.

Source: *Two Hours with Tilly*, Alison Peters.

Thomas was not happy with his father. Tick the box next to the statement which tells why he was upset.

Thomas was upset with his dad because ...

a) he decided that his father was not worth talking to. ☐

b) he didn't like the way his dad spoke to him. ☐

c) he had to walk a long way to where he was going. ☐

d) his dad had to work on Saturday and couldn't go with him. ☐

Colour the statement that best tells how Dad felt about leaving Thomas.

Thomas' dad was not happy about leaving him because ...	a) he was going to miss out on the fun.
	b) he had to work on a Saturday.
	c) he felt he had let Thomas down.
	d) he was afraid Thomas may get lost.

Thomas thought, "On our Saturday afternoon". Colour the statement that best explains why he thought this.

a) Thomas spent time with his father every Saturday after-noon. He expected this Saturday to be the same.

b) Thomas thought that he may have to walk home because his dad wasn't going to be there with him.

c) Thomas did not like his father working all the time.

ASSESSMENT

Fires that burn in the bush or forest are known as bushfires, or forest fires. Small fires have benefits (are good) for plants and soil, but severe fires damage the environment for years. If fires burn out of control, they can also destroy ___________.

Source: Go Facts, *Fire and Drought*, Blake Education.

In many places in the bush and along roads there are signs that warn about bushfires. Shade the round sign that best gives people a warning about bushfires.

- Do Not Light Fires Here!
- Bushfires Kill! Do NOT Light Fires!
- Bushfires May Be Dangerous!

Explain why you chose the bushfire sign you shaded.

____

____

New Sploosh Head Lice Treatment

Applied once before bedtime, this amazing head lice treatment gets rid of these revolting creatures almost magically!

Dangerous chemicals in other treatments may have terrible effects on the long-term health of children. They are poisonous and dangerous.

Parents, don't endanger your children – use Sploosh!

What may parents infer from reading this advertisement? Shade the star of the sentence that says this best.

a) Sploosh is better than other lotions.	☆
b) Sploosh doesn't contain dangerous chemicals and is better.	☆
c) Sploosh may remove head lice.	☆

ASSESSMENT

TARGETING COMPREHENSION 4 © PASCAL PRESS ISBN 9781925490633

Ocean pollution and overfishing are major problems. People need to work together to protect the oceans of the world.

Whatever people put down a drain also ends up in the ocean. Even chemical sprays used on farms can seep through the ground and end up in the ocean.

Source: Go Facts, *People and the Sea*, Blake Education.

Read the text and write one reason why we should protect our oceans.

____

____

____

Eventually, governments will pass laws to protect oceans. What is happening now may be stopped in the future. Shade the headline which may be printed in newspapers when this happens.

OVERFISHING NO CAUSE FOR CONCERN	OCEANS REMAIN IN SOME DANGER	BANS IMPOSED ON DUMPING CHEMICALS DOWN DRAINS

The use of mobile phones by children **MUST** be **banned**. Doctors have found proof that mobile phones are **VERY dangerous** because of their unseen radio waves. However, it is safe for children to use a mobile phone for a short time if they really need to. **Overuse is DANGEROUS!**

What do you predict parents would do if their child really needed to use a mobile phone? Shade your answer.

a)	Parents would not let their child use a mobile phone for any reason.
b)	Parents would make all calls and texts for their child instead.
c)	Parents would allow their child to use their phone for emergencies.

ASSESSMENT

Predicting

Eliza heard the music of the ice-cream van. She couldn't ask her mum for some money before it drove away because Aunty Patsy was busy talking. Dad was changing channels on the TV so quickly that no-one could watch it.

To top it all off, her brother Eric blew his nose and then chased her around the house trying to rub his hanky in her face.

Eliza then slipped on a half-sucked mango Eric had dropped in the dining room. She slid across the tiles into the display cabinet. Just when Eliza thought she had avoided disaster, it toppled over, smashing half of her mother's best plates.

Into a large shopping bag, Eliza packed all the clothes she could fit, two muesli bars and a packet of chicken noodle soup mix. She loaded the bag onto her bike, along with her birthday presents — a skateboard and Superstar Barbie campervan. She balanced her hula hoop on her shoulders and pedalled off down the hill, towards …

Source: Sparklers, *Running Away*, Blake Education. [abridged]

4 Shade the statement that best predicts what may have happened next.

- Eliza decided to go hide in the bush for a couple of days.
- Eliza's Aunt Patsy saw her and took her home.
- Having so many things on her bike, she fell off at the bottom of the hill.

Spices were valuable in the Middle Ages because their use in cooking was a sign of wealth and high social position. Pepper, nutmeg, cinnamon and saffron added flavour.

People used spices to treat headaches, fevers and bad breath. People also preserved meat with spices because there was no refrigeration.

Source: Go Facts, *Explorers*, Blake Education.

5 Spices have been used in cooking for hundreds of years. Why are they so popular? Circle your answer.

- They are cheap to buy.
- They add colour and flavour, and have health benefits.
- Spicy food helps people live longer.

ASSESSMENT

TARGETING COMPREHENSION 4 © PASCAL PRESS ISBN 9781925490633

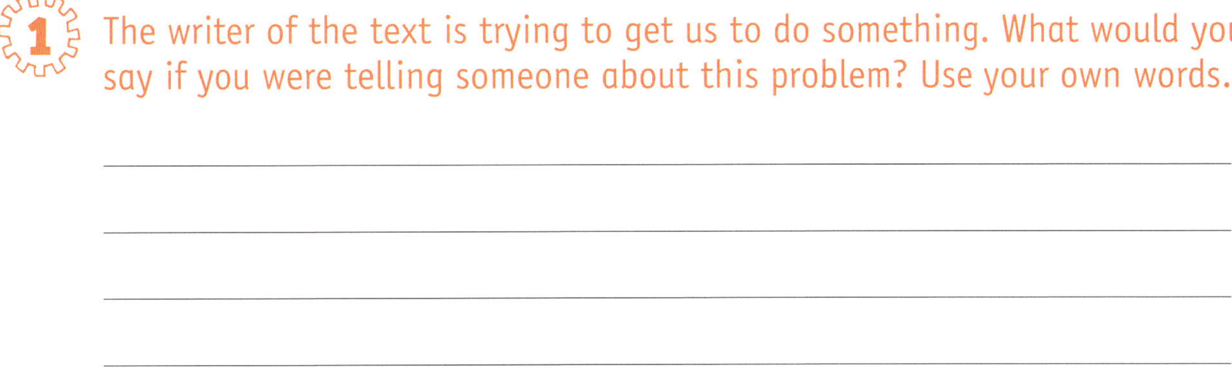

People are killing our oceans. Everyone **must** take action and do something because we are **murdering** sea creatures. Rubbish dumped on the ground by lazy people ends up as a poison in the fish we eat.

No-one wants to kill our planet! No-one wants to see whales die out! No-one wants to swim in stinking water! You, yes you, need to act now!

1 The writer of the text is trying to get us to do something. What would you say if you were telling someone about this problem? Use your own words.

____

____

____

____

People who light fires during summer are incredibly stupid! People may be hurt or worse! Bushfires can also cause damage to property.

Could you live with yourself if someone died because of a fire you had started? Would you feel proud if houses were burnt and animals killed because of your actions? How would you feel if it was your house?

The writer wrote this text to send a particular message. Shade the box that best explains this message.

The writer wanted to tell readers about the danger of bushfires in summer.

The writer wanted readers to know that it is stupid to light fires in summer that could cause bushfires, threatening people, homes and property.

ASSESSMENT

Analysing

Every year, people hold thousands of different celebrations around the world. Special days celebrate things we value and help us remember the past. Some celebrations have been around for thousands of years. For example, the first known celebration of Christmas was in the year 336.

Other celebrations are newer. Japanese people celebrated Mountain Day for the first time in 2016. It is a day to "get closer to mountains and to appreciate the benefits of mountains."

Australia's Harmony Day celebrates living in a country with people from many different backgrounds. It celebrates the values of belonging and respect.

Source: Go Facts, *World Celebrations*, Blake Education.

3 Which one of the following statements best explains Australian ideals (ways of acting and thinking)?

Most Australians feel that ...

a) people are welcome in our country but we don't try to understand where they come from. ☐

b) people coming to our country should adopt Australian ideals and forget their past. ☐

c) newcomers should give up their beliefs and cultures because they are in a new country. ☐

d) everyone should be respected and given a fair go as we share and celebrate our different cultures. ☐

Milly had done everything to make kids at her new school like her. Practical jokes, like pulling a chair out from underneath someone as they were about to sit, were really funny. Teasing someone was really clever she thought.

No-one ever got angry with her at home when she did this. Her family just laughed and said, "Oh, that's just Milly being Milly."

4 Milly's behaviour would have been seen differently at her new school by other students. Shade the sentence that best tells about this.

Milly's parents would be happy with the way she was acting at school.	Other students would have seen her behaving that way and they would behave the same way.	Milly would have been seen as a bully by other students.

ASSESSMENT

TARGETING COMPREHENSION 4 © PASCAL PRESS ISBN 9781925490633

There are only a few more weeks of school before the long holidays. We spend the hottest part of the day at school waiting for the final bell to ring. Then we rush home.

Every afternoon, I throw my bag down, grab something to eat and then meet up with Jah, my friend, as quickly as possible. The sun won't set for hours and there is always heaps to do.

Source: Sparklers, *The Great Race*, Blake Education. [abridged]

One of the statements below tells about the time of year the story is set in. Tick the box next to the statement which is true.

The story takes place ...

a) in summer, just before the Christmas holidays. ☐

b) at the end of the school holidays in January. ☐

c) just before winter in May. ☐

d) just before the Easter holidays at the end of the first school term. ☐

Tasmanian tigers are the enemy of every farmer in the colony. These brutal beasts rip our stock apart in the dark of the night. Killing these savage creatures can only make life easier for everyone and ensure the safety of our stock.

Tasmanian tigers have now been extinct for nearly a century. Because silly farmers were fearful of losing stock, these animals were hunted and slaughtered needlessly. Thoughtlessly, these people ignored the future.

The texts above have very different ideas about Tasmanian Tigers. Shade the sentence which best tells of these differences.

a) The first text says that Tasmanian tigers were dangerous. The second text says that Tasmanian tigers weren't a danger.
b) The first text is saying that the killing of Tasmanian tigers should not have happened. The second text agrees with this idea.
c) The first text tells why Tasmanian tigers were killed. The second text disagrees and says that these animals were killed for little reason.

ASSESSMENT

Tornadoes, also called twisters, are revolving (turning) funnels of air that stretch from storm clouds to the ground. Tornadoes can suck up anything from cows and cars, to barns and combine harvesters.

In Tornado Alley, people build shelters near their homes. They watch the skies and listen to the radio for warnings during tornado season.

Source: Go Facts, *Wild Weather*, Blake Education. [abridged]

Read the text about the dangers of tornadoes. Shade the statement that best gives the main idea of the text.

a) During tornadoes trees may lose their leaves and not look very nice.	☆
b) Houses can be smashed. Cars and farm machinery can be destroyed and people killed.	☆
c) People sit around listening to their radios and don't do any work.	☆
d) People are in danger during tornadoes and hide in shelters to protect themselves.	☆

A leathery, black creature poked out from beneath the rotting log. Its thin flickering tongue searched the air. The movement caught Kevin's eye.

"No, it couldn't be a snake. Perhaps a lizard?" he thought. Curved claws scraped aside the leaves, and the furry, funnel-shaped head appeared in full.

Just an __________ sniffing out some termites. Kevin relaxed now that he knew it wasn't a snake.

Source: Sparklers, *Kevin's* _________, Blake Education.

In this text Kevin decides that this animal is definitely not a snake. Write the **first** words that give Kevin's reason for knowing the animal was not a snake or lizard.

____

ASSESSMENT

Too much money is spent on cyclone shelters! Building them is a waste of money and time because cyclones don't happen every day.

How silly are people, spending money for no reason? Sure, you need to take care. Moving into a safe room should be enough. As usual, people panic about nothing, a total waste of time.

Why not spend the money on something useful like painting the house? As usual, crazy people are being quite ridiculous about something that may never happen.

1 What are some things people could do to prepare for a cyclone? Clue: Remember that cyclones have very strong winds and very heavy rain.

2 Most people would not agree with the ideas in the persuasive text above. Explain why they would not agree with some of the ideas.

Shattered after her sprint from danger, Melanie collapsed, out of breath and crying behind a tree stump. Camping in the forest wasn't supposed to be like this. The booklet said that bears always stayed clear of people. Anger at the thought of being put into danger began to …

3 Write what you think Melanie was angry about.

ASSESSMENT

La Tomatina (late August): A celebration where thousands of people throw tomatoes at each other.

Tunarama (Australia Day weekend): A festival of tuna in Port Lincoln, South Australia, including a tuna tossing competition.

Cooper's Hill Cheese-Rolling Festival (late May): People chase a large wheel of cheese as it rolls down a hill in Gloucestershire, England.

Source: Go Facts, *World Celebrations*, Blake Education.

Each of these occasions celebrates food in a totally different way. What was the thought behind these festivals? Shade the thought bubble that you think is accurate.

a) Let's just waste food and have a great day. Yahoo!

b) What a way to get the tourists to come — a food fight!

c) We are so lucky. We should celebrate this great year.

d) Let's celebrate a great season and a great deal of food. People may come and join in.

Polar Bear Plunge Day (1 January): People jump into freezing water. Popular in the United States, Canada, United Kingdom and the Netherlands.

Source: Go Facts, *World Celebrations*, Blake Education.

Why couldn't this tradition happen in Australia on the date mentioned above? Colour the sun beside the correct answer.

a) Countries that celebrate this day are very cold and have snow and ice.	
b) It is summer in Australia at this time of year.	
c) Australia doesn't have a really cold winter in most places. Ice doesn't form in rivers.	

ASSESSMENT